The Deletions

AKRON SERIES IN POETRY

For a complete listing of titles published in the series,
go to www.uakron.edu/uapress/poetry

The Deletions

Sarah Green

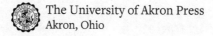
The University of Akron Press
Akron, Ohio

ISBN: 978-1-62922-300-1 (paper)
ISBN: 978-1-62922-301-8 (ePDF)
ISBN: 978-1-62922-302-5 (ePub)

A catalog record for this title is available from the Library of Congress.

∞ The paper used in this publication meets the minimum requirements of ANSI/NISO
z39.48–1992 (Permanence of Paper).

Cover image: Kylie Gellatly, *Flood Damage* (2024). Cover design by Amy Freels.

The Deletions was designed and typeset in FreightText Pro with FreightSans Pro titles by
Amy Freels and printed on fifty-five-pound natural.

Produced in conjunction with the University
of Akron Affordable Learning Initiative.
More information is available at
www.uakron.edu/affordablelearning

For Lizzie and Jack

Contents

III.

I.

Matter

Today I touched lilacs
as if I was saying *wait* with my fingers,
tugging a shirt so the person inhabiting it
would turn to me. I don't know who I was
pulling back from the other world. Maybe
my friend who died, the one I dreamed

walked past the line of torches on the beach
marking that property from this, past a sign
he did not care about. It was only for me.
Maybe I touched him—but I don't believe
we become everything. He's not the same
as the flower. He is somewhere,

and I'm grateful that I don't understand
because it means I'm still alive: stupid, partial,
desiring specific ways of feeling good,
crying on the couch because it's light so late
and the birds won't stop singing. It's light,
and it doesn't matter what I want.

Blueberries for Sal

Each year there seem to be fewer blueberries in the lot
at the top of the hill, purple or green, small as a bead
lost from a string when the baby reached for it
and broke the whole necklace,

laughing. You remember the way your thighs bruised
under his one-year-old sneakers, and your jaw blew up in hives,
your nipples bled. That's a lie. You remember

raspberries at the side of the road when it was just sand,
gravel to slip down on the steep return. Wild strawberries
in the dirt driveway, growing along the grass mohawk
between the tires. You grow confused, think you were Sal.

You think you saw the bear in the story.
You think you're thawing cans of Minute Maid for some child,
but you're the child, you're the one mixing the dough,

wiping your hands on the apron that is your grandmother's.
You wash the berries in her colander. You turn to teach
someone what to do next, but it's just you, putting the key back
where it goes, closing the gate, taking the right

at the gully, turning to check for a boat one more time
that won't be there.

Two Months in to the Separation,
I Write *Best*

and he writes *cheers*
as if we have never gone after each other's bodies
on the living room couch as if there was just this

//

one chance   with the blinds open
the mailman almost done next door
in the obscene bright middle of the day

—just enough time before kid pickup

//

as if it never felt like a psalm
and wasn't it? The way we'd rise, survey

the aftermath,
our victory   as if no one ever had it
                this good—

Lago Trasimeno

Every so often I think of that leg of prosciutto
Hanging by a string off the back of the door
At my friend's wedding in that other country,
Our mid-twenties

Each time the door opened, I thought about germs
As the prosciutto like a pendulum
Swayed on its string and knocked against the wood

You are getting very sleepy
You are among groves
You are wearing a black silk dress

Groomsman 1 brings you to a room with lit candles
Around the bed where you are meant to lie
But Groomsman 3 keeps banging on the door
Because he forgot his wallet
Which is just as well
Because the bride looks so pale in these photographs
Your flip phone captured at the eight-course meal
And an Italian says the prosciutto should not have been sold

You are not aged   You are not cured
You and the bride and the prosciutto

You are so young, even blood-orange juice surprises you

Every so often I think of it

Lost Button

Because my beige jacket button,
already lost once and recovered under the radiator
to be sewn on again, has been misplaced
a second time, I'm coming apart,
running my hand under cushions, catching my palm
on the ready needle, with its maddening line
of pale blue thread. Today's moving
quickly. The sun over the salt marsh is a record
winding down. And that missing girl—

they've got her face xeroxed
in every restaurant doorway. Freckled and seventeen,
with long blonde hair. Are they always
blonde? She's smiling like a ghost. In the Maine newsstands,
her mother squints, front page, smoking.
The photo stacked against itself
so many times, you'd think that cigarette would
burn right through.

I hear a lobsterman found her car.
I know by now they've buried her, closing the library
with the white hydrangeas in front for the afternoon.
The helicopters parked back in their lot.
But I keep seeing her in the river,
gathering every lost thing. Her good news
waiting like a penny on her tongue.

Arrhythmias

The internet says *an excitable rhythm can be reset*
by sleeping next to a calm one.
But I'm in a long-distance relationship, and—

remember your twenties? The way Alicia Keys
drew out the word *falling*—
that's what my heart does late at night.

A stranger in Bangalore tracks the monitor.
The Mars Rover is not afraid, I heard the Canadian
astronaut say on air to a small boy.

Because it's doing what it loves, and that is exploring.
The boy and I have been having trouble sleeping.
The boy had been afraid

that it would break. It would break far away,
and there would be no one to repair it.
The astronaut says *I am convinced the Mars Rover*
                    is a happy machine. Do you feel better now?

Boston Harbor

The featured pop star's voice was too big for the waterfront
pavilion. That's what the reviewer said. Her recent poignant hit
flew overhead, drifted right out of open sides

of the white tent, somehow tugging us with it, flinging us toward stars
where we hung briefly before falling among jellyfish and buoys.
Once we were part of the water, we couldn't also take it in.

The folk singer who opened for her, meanwhile, was just a small light
making a proportional circle—his song meant for historic basements
whose walls make a story's echoes ricochet back into hearts

of customers at small tables, who debrief on the train after, rating
the concert on the persistence of its shrapnel. Sometimes I am not vast
enough to match the love

that takes the form of sky and railroad tracks,
canyon and breeze. I am down here, solo, shooting arrows
into some clouds after a drought. And you're

the clouds making me sweat, and the arrow's trajectory,
and the idea of the field.

Diorama

Mid-morning, blackout
curtains drawn, our glowing bed's
almost the size of this small room.

And you at the center—you
remind me of the geode on my desk
pinning a note I'll come back to.

We've arranged everything.

A painting full of blues and greens,
a woman's back, her hair gathered,
one hand holding it there.

But I keep wondering who's out singing
Laura Nyro, maybe two houses down.
Is it the grown daughter again,
hosing a blaze of dark roses—?

Fifty Things Kids Can Do To Save the Earth

Here comes today's lead dove again, cooing. There goes the
  countryside.

When I was a city kid on summer nights I'd hear men yell and break
bottles, but I never saw them. Three flights up, my mother's pie plate

balanced in the windowsill. I guess I'm grown. When I hear a dove

sing like a bruise, I think: if I could just turn into ice. I think: I should
  make
myself useful. But for entire stretches

this afternoon, even with air conditioning, I was so hot, so querulous,

all I could do was lie. The dove off sleeping or hunting…I envy it, so
  light
it doesn't harm a single power line. Not to brag, but I can't touch one
  wire

without bringing entire forests down. A new species extinct each day

whether or not I plant my tree, and it makes me unsure
where to stand. Like a bride, I keep stepping on my dress, but everyone
  says

It can be fixed! This is your day!

Foreshadowing

The ash tree is sick and has to be cut down.
The string lights break.

The handsome mayor's begun to lose
the people's confidence.

A squirrel runs in circles and falls over.
The lost dog won't let me tether it.

Our neighbor strips on his porch,
out of his mind.

The monarch with the deformed wing
does not live happily among the zinnias
like I promised the children.

Look—one hydrangea's blooming
in two different colors.

A man sleeps next to me
like pillows put there to resemble a man
who is right here, keeping his vow.

Vortex, Amtrak

Bright scab of track.
Bright stitch each train
rips out. In negative

degrees, metal cowers
as if a god had threatened
to curse it,

and did. Freezes. Mends
wrong. Can never get
the trick, never can jump.

(Crowd gets its money
back.) Despite
each kerosene-soaked rope

laid down. Despite lions
of flame.

II.

Nike

An elegy for my student Raychand, 17

He says: Poet, I spy
a water tower
abandoned by clouds

I squint a cigarette
you think I can't see
from this hill on G street

bricks like 5x close up
slides of skin
I spy

empty half gallons
tied to trees
crevice silt no rain

Do I feel like a crevice?
I feel like an eye
for a bright sneaker

an eye easily winning
your game
I feel wind finally

rustling the T-shirt
at my back here in sweat city
and I see color

do you? I see my color
and its color somehow even
with no eyes behind my head

no hands no bike no mother
who can carry everything I win

The Afterlife

1.

This must be what morning sickness feels like:
pushing a spinach omelet around my plate across the table
from a boy who maybe got me pregnant. I was a virgin yesterday.

It's a long weekend in Ohio—

I've swallowed pills a friend of a friend's doctor gave her for
emergencies. I trust her, because she's someone who once
asked the universe to give her a guitar, and she has a guitar now.

2.

The pills work—I'm not pregnant. The boy takes a bus
back to his life, and I go out to dinner with my father.
He has cancer. It's newly June. Mussels are heaped on a plate.

New wet leaves on the trees are shivering like prom dresses.
How grown-up I feel suddenly: somebody a baby could mistake
for a mother. Somebody whose father could die.

3.

But my father will live. Is this when I begin to catch the eye
of the gods? Is this when they mark me for not having paid?

4.

Thirty-four, working my way through a punch card for candlelight
yoga, falling through space. Darkness lapping
at my wrists and my ankles. That afternoon, my boyfriend,

a father already, had said—like he was reading tarot—he couldn't
see us having a child. Like I'd drawn the card

for the hanged man.
Class was winding down. Soon, everyone would spray
their mats. But I was sprawled on a deck,
a fish someone had cut with a sharp blade down the middle.
On my left side, life waiting. My own baby. On my right—

how could I let love go now that I'd finally found it? The knife
sliced through. I chose both. Neither. How to explain
that I'm still there—late September, corpse pose? And the rest
of this—now—is the afterlife?

5.

In the afterlife, I can't decide, so I go to a clinic
that promises a "snapshot of fertility."

The lab says my ovaries are stones.
Stones with the imprint of ferns, yes.
But only the imprint.

They say last year I could have—

but my body skipped like a record.
The pretty doctor in leopard print shoes says
there's no hurry anymore.

No follicles.
The ultrasound's a cloudy night.

7.

Still, I am trying to return.

The acupuncturist pierces my ear cartilage and my uterus leaps.

I have *ovarian failure.*
It is unexplained. I ask the expert about his anecdotes
of remission. Is it like a radio station

coming in and out? And he says, *it's more like the weather.*

The acupuncturist says there is grief in my lungs.

I read the study about platelet-rich plasma.
I read the study about the self-healing provoked by bee stings.
And more good news

> *the women's ovaries were removed and cut into strips, which were*
> *frozen.*
> *Later the strips were thawed and cut into tiny cubes.*
> *The cubes were transplanted.*

But I don't want my ovaries cut into cubes. Do you know what I mean?

That is not part of the birth stories the tipsy moms tell in the treehouse
under the stars over a kid's zipline.

7.

I want to be a tipsy mom in the treehouse under the stars.
And if not—

8.

Regret like a car alarm that follows me
through neighborhoods?

No one to tell about the ancestors?

9.

There must be a place where I don't have to remember feeling
the possibility of meteors.

How does one sneak out of the afterlife?

How can I stay in this body? How can I withstand the future's
choose-your-own chapters in which I always fail

10.

to make something?

It's what a mother would do—stay.

11.

The Dalai Lama says we've all been each other's mothers
too many times to even count.

But I only remember this lifetime.

Runaway

I was fifteen. My father and I stood
at the basement threshold
shouting at each other—
one of the last times. *Go,* he said.
Get out. He propped the screen door
with the back of his body.

And I left, slipping
that house over my head in the slow
dream anger can be. Ran down
the drive, deaf from the blood traffic
of my heartbeat, past the azaleas, down
the bike path, until I had to stop

to breathe. Just then I thought
I heard my name, my brother calling
from our street. But I was wrong.
No one was home. So it fell to the rose trellis
to shelter me, disguising me as its shadow.

Lorain County, 1999

The driver says *You're lucky you got me. Some other guy*—He stops.
Cornfields press in.

The road unspools: cassette gone wrong, just ribboning.
I would hate to see you

raped and strangled in a ditch. I would hate to see your throat bruised
and your eyes wild. I would hate to see you jogging, flushed with
  endorphins—

onto the highway's stretch of trees, their change this fall the color
of weak tea, as if they didn't have the energy—

with headphones on when out of nowhere someone holds a knife to you.
I would hate to hold a knife to you.

I would hate to have to—
airport signs—*you're lucky. You are so lucky.*

Women's Studies

1.

In this storyline, I am the bread maker
for the vegetarian co-op. My shift's ended.
My wet apron hangs over the sink.

I've left the metal bowl, rinsed out each part
of the machine. It's dusk. I'm almost home.

Enter: a scratch in the record, a clattering
that can't be placed, a man lifting away
a window screen to climb into the basement

where my bread is still cooling.
He's putting something heavy in his hand.

2.

It could have been any of us. Once upstairs,
he tried the door to every dorm room,

wielding the same blunt hook I'd used to mix
the water and flour. But the half-killed girl

woke up. Later, she'd say: *I prayed
the rosary out loud. Prayed for his soul.* He ran—

3.

I was asleep in my friend Lucy's bed.

Her freckles tasted like tea tree soap.
I used to say things to her in my mind
while I kissed her.

4.

This was our second week of school.
That girl dropped out by October.

Lucy set her radio to Natalie Merchant
so we'd wake up
to march and chant at four a.m.

Take back the night! the flyers said.

But it's years later, and the night
still belongs to men.

Kanyakumari

And now I'm thinking, it doesn't matter
if that palm reader in Kanyakumari—

a city famous for its beach sunrise, to which we took a train
so we could sleep over the night before a rare occurrence
of thick clouds—was right about any of it.

The foreign royalty my friend would marry.
How soon I'd die.

At twenty, she and I had already read each other's palms
a dozen times.

We were prepared for death or love. Maybe our true fortune
was how we'd charm and fight our way out after
that stranger led us past silk bolts to his back room.

Lines on Trees

Lines on the trees mark how the flood once rose
over our heads. And now there's something only half
of each tree knows. I'm twenty-two, I am submerged
in the swell of watching this butch on a ladder—

shaved head, tattoos, and a tank top—fixing the bulb
over my door. When my knees get weak, I make a note:
it doesn't just happen in songs. I'll kiss her in basements
where she takes a break from cutting boxes with a knife

to pull me in by the belt loops, and I'll kiss her at rush hour
at night in Indiana where it's still dangerous.
And in the morning in Indiana. It is still legal to smoke
around us at the diner where I will order

a vegetarian omelet, and they will not know what I mean.
What they will bring is just egg with lettuce inside it.
And I will laugh. But when my students ask why I'm not
married, I'll make up a boyfriend to throw them off.

And when she invites me to walk farther down to the river,
I'll say I'm wearing the wrong shoes.

Chance Creek

for Emma Howell

Better to shut your eyes
for the daredevil walk on this rusted-out bridge beam.

Remember? We've done it in our sleep, Emma.
We've done it drunk and high.

But you're distracted by orchards and the blood
on your left heel—listen, there's no need
to grip the rail like that.

Emma, come on—

this afternoon's not when you die.
Today in muddy Ohio, a net we don't know about
is drifting down the creek.

If you could cup next summer to your ear,
you'd hear the heart murmur of waves lifting
your body, the trawlers shouting, echoing.

But for now, you're nineteen, intent on a toehold,
eager for a swim. You steady yourself, frown.
Emma, I take it

      back. Take your time.

Ursa Major

My therapist's face says *you will never know me*
Like it's a triumph while he turns
Into one ex-boyfriend after another,
Reading a book he bought in Japan,
Cooking a meal his new girlfriend likes,
Shaving in the half-light. I'm just the laundry
Hung between the windows, strung
By a line connecting all the men to each other
In their insistence on living outside of my lens,
Speaking off-stage, thinking their thoughts
Where I cannot follow. But all I want is to follow
On my blue bicycle with its basket and tassels,
Its loud bell, calling to them to look, saying *listen*.
Like the neighbor's kid who needs someone to see her
Handsprings in the green backyard. *These are
No thoughts for a child*, the men who leave me behind say,
So I become a man. I put away childish things.
I live in a small apartment facing the sea, and I stack cups
In a way that pleases me. I have a dictionary and a radio.
I changed my address; I don't know how longing found me
And seeped toward me like moonlight or the sound
Of strangers fucking through a wall. I don't know who
I want to be when I hear them. I just walk out,
An obvious target for arrows, into the foreign square,
The familiar beloved lonely square I can never translate
To my therapist, with the harpist playing
For change and the telescope unlocked by change
And the chalk artist, his upturned hat ready.
Which one are you, I ask my therapist, but he says
He does not exist, is just a constellation I saw in the dark
And called an animal. He says, *Which one are you?*

Plus-One: Falmouth

I wasn't sure who I was.
I was in my thirties. I looked for clues in the bride's childhood
bookshelf: *My Side of the Mountain, Summer of My German Soldier.*
I picked up figurines. The dust below them seemed like mine.
I lay down on her chenille bed.

Downstairs, flowers were arriving.
I speared a block of cheese from the fruit plate.
I'd come by train to buzz around the side of a wine glass.
I mean I coveted and didn't know how to get to
sweetness. There was a beach, and a man on the guest list
had invited me to everything but the party. I remember him
beckoning me, closing the door.

After we used the bride's towels,
we dressed again in view of maple trees, their new leaves
blindly rushing to happen.

Everyone left for the church.
I walked through that vacant beach town until I found the one
part of the stage set (painted lilacs, mural of silhouettes) I could
actually knock on and open.

Up by the register, among the scalloped edge postcards—
Dear Mrs. Gillespie—
I looked for someone who missed me. *Does Mr. Gillespie
object to me writing to you?* I looked for someone who would
tell me to come home.

Lariat

for Bill

When your friends and I gathered for the rumble,
snapping our fingers, feeling for our switchblades,

that was your memorial. I was ready to shove you

against a wall, knock you out, for knocking yourself
so permanently out, and all of us, off our winged feet,

roping us in, while you rode away, masked man.

But on this warm day, late October—even the shadows
lush against white blinds, gold and red leaves eddying

before settling on the road—I fold my coat

under one arm and think of what you're missing, here,
in our windblown, scribbled equation of a world. Even

after so much reading, maybe you didn't know

everything yet. You could have used that rope to lead
a colt. Thrown it just in time for a boy fallen through ice.

Could have knotted yourself a bridge to come back on.

Tinder Bio

a cento of lines from the dating app profiles of Minnesota men

Wild days and trouble are mostly behind me.
All of my pictures were taken in the past. That's how pictures work.
The way to win me over is: Give me a pasture where there can be
    anything inside.
I once dressed up as Moses.
I need someone to come over and make me a box of shells and cheese.
I'm tired of coming home to an empty house.
I am a Turkish Prince. I'm sort of like a deer: wild & free; gentle, yet
Love my life, won't settle, must see stars.
I don't smoke, and I don't gamble. I am simple.
Are you okay with awkward silences?
Will you join me at the dog park?
Looking for a connection so powerful it brings me to my knees.
I enjoy so many things, including things I haven't even discovered yet.
Life is a vibe. Everyone has been through, or is going through, things.
Looking for that "you've never met anyone like me" vibe.
I think I'm doing this wrong.
To be perfectly honest, my life is okay.
I don't know a lot, but I do know a lot, you know?
I've made mistakes. I'm not gonna be your first choice.
Can we skip to the part where we're comfortable in silence with one
    another?
You remember Prince Charming? Yeah, that's not me.
I'm probably not as supportive as you'd like.
I believe in music the way some people believe in fairy tales.
I build boxes with exotic woods.
Jeremy is my real name.

The Auditions

The auditions disappointed me personally. All of the women could breathe fire. All of the men could disappear. Sharp knives available to juggle were too safe. China plates to be balanced on palms of dancers on ponies' spines turned out to be unbreakable. After the applicants had gone home and I'd poured my bourbon, twin tiger cubs raced orangely toward me. They knocked me over with greetings. From the circus floor I cursed in a warm tone. *Stupid Peace,* I growled. *Stupid Tenderness.*

Tower Park

The ache of watching sledders every winter
from the same window

inside my mother's house was once an ache
to have a dad who would watch me.

And then it was an ache to bring a child to the hill
to take our turns.

But now I'm beyond that.

Where have I been?
Am I the fox at the park's edge?

Grass where the snow's worn off?
I watch the sleds,

and I'm no human in the scene.

III.

The Deletions

"Thousands Petition Junior Dictionary over Nature Words."
—BBC

Now that they're scrapping *acorn* and *heron*,
I know you're next, *cygnet*—
kid I was saving those words for.

Someone in charge of the dictionary's real estate
is tearing out *bluebell* and *cowslip*,
paving the outskirts

where I thought I'd find you
studying berries. You are why I've pressed
leaves. Why I've looked up

what kind of bird. I wanted to show you
the wild carrot at the root of Queen Anne's lace.
How the familiar hides in far soil.

Can you get here soon? They're saying *kingfisher*
is losing relevance. Will our future be like
when Odysseus visited *a land that knows nothing*

of the sea, and its inhabitants mistook his oar
for a winnowing fan? Were they thinking of battle
or sin, the men who first studied in women

the slow breakdown of viable eggs
and called it *attrition*? The deletions take *otter*
and *pasture*. You must exist
somewhere words go when their world's gone.

My Liver

The masked and blue-gowned man
with the needle in my liver
says, when I ask if I can breathe normally,
breathe beautifully

/

after, he asks me to spell *vague*

/

and I think he thinks I'm sedated but I am just
awake saying hi to everyone like usual except
there's iodine on my torso
there's lidocaine in my feelings
on a whiteboard
someone has reproduced a Norwegian painting
in dry erase.   with blue and black markers

(of his process, the artist wrote,
I *sensed a scream passing through nature—*)

/

and when I start to feel faint,

I say, thinking of lovers who've coaxed me to briefly exit
my body, *praise me*,
knowing how far I'd go for approval, pain's antidote

/

my friend texts to ask
if I'm going to our high school reunion,
and when I tell her I'm waiting for a biopsy she writes:

perhaps it will help to know that liver in Farsi is a love organ.
Like, when you see a cute baby you say "my liver"
or "I'm going to eat your liver"

/

holding me there, drugged by my own longing, he says
you're doing so great   we should make a video to show
other patients the click   the ache   a piece of me missing

You Were Already Good

Tearing the pages, taping medieval bodices of
girls meadows fractals of sunlight on your wall,
the copy something like "much ado about

summer"—already good sleeping under Jim Morrison,
beads and bare chest, his/yours, the cheap foam of
headphones hurting your ear. Spit on the pillow. Already

before the rope bridge over whitewater to a house
that could only be built by teenagers like you
over spring break, in West Virginia, where you got so mad

at something you've forgotten now, you broke
the handle off the kitchen sink. The medicine didn't
keep you from crying,

did it? Just made you sunburn easily. Still you were good
at the night vigil on Holy Saturday falling asleep in a chair,
trying not to, holding a small cup of grape juice. Awake,

surprised you didn't once spill it. Good even if you had,
although you weren't baptized, which is how you ended up
in the river. That's when Jane took you into her own hands.

The Mower in the Dew

1.

Waiting for someone?

The Olive Garden waiter asked. White linen napkin over his arm,
he stood. Taking that seriously. Believing in his wine.

But my friend had died.

All that day and one day earlier I couldn't open a door without
   thinking a body
might be draped behind it.

Although that was unreasonable.

2.

When today I dropped my quarter for the meter
in some underbrush, the wind picked up,
spitting pink and white petals, and I remembered

a flurry around us at your funeral. Weren't you—
Bill—already planning it the last time I ran into you?

We were at the convenience store. Weren't you down
to your last light? When we walked out, you agreed:
a pretty moon. Seems to me now you swiftly bound

and gagged that moon, throwing it into the water
so—in the dark—you could proceed.

3.

At the memorial, someone went on about the *Nietzschean yes.*

Someone said Bill taught her the word *Kairos.*

I remembered how, during class, he would not let himself sneeze.
His face would turn red as he withheld it.

One of the last things he said to me was *you don't need to dye your hair.*

Our teacher remembered the last paper he wrote was about the
    loneliness
of the little unmown strip of butterfly weed Frost's speaker finds.

4.

Still just us three.

We joked that the waiter was interested in me.

I ordered the pesto chicken ravioli.

Will someone be joining you? he asked, once more,

like the answer might change.

Stick Figure

The girl in math class
skips to the answers. And as she
thumbs through, a stick figure
in pencil down by the page numbers
raises an arm, a leg. Spidery kicks.
She thinks, *somebody did all of that*
work instead of listening.

Never two parents at one time,
not even when, all three of them
raking, she holds the flimsy bag
while they take turns
tamping leaves down. Her mother
blames her when the leaves drift out.
Her dad wavers like smoke.
Still in work clothes.

When the wind blows, her father
hears the geese honking,
imagines one drops like a plane,
grabs at his shirt. Lifts off
with him. Rooftops, chimneys...

He is too sad to feel
ridiculous up there, his tie flapping,
the v spacing apart
making a place for him
as if this happens every day.

Vines

My mother wrestles with the stakes
and I with her, with the tomato vines
caught in our decades-old wires.
Their stalks threaten to split
as the wires tangle.

And we blame everything—the heat,
the mosquitoes bearing some new,
life-threatening disease—for our hot-
headedness. Apologize over cool drinks
later. It's like this every year.

Always, a plant's already fallen
past repair. *Oh well,* I think. *Still time,*
says my mother, who built the fence
and the raised bed, planted because
something should be alive each year

while we die back. Alive beyond what
we can tend, though we tend it—
rather, my mother does, without saying
if she regrets having children. I think
she doesn't regret it. Although

at twenty-nine she thought it would be
criminal to bring me here just to fall
prey, or out of love, or asleep at the wheel
while she is teaching me to drive
the dawn.

Evidence

Lizzie, who's eight, says *Mom, I'm going out!*
and grabs her keys—
toy ones she's had since she was a baby.

Now she's sixteen. Freedom's a magnet she thrills to.
And: scene. This round, she wants to play the mom.
She packs my lunch. All of this time, singing her songs

in the bath, fetching a water glass at night, I think
I'm childless. Kicking the ball, *childless.* Watching her
bellow with joy at the top of a hill.

Later, we sweep leaves off the back path so it's clear.
How quickly wind fills it in. I want to grab
the stepmother I was, and say: *Look at her: your family.*

By next summer, I'll be so young, I will not even be
married. Save for some iris bulbs, a scruff of
strawberries, there'll be no evidence that we lived here.

Moving Day

Strangers descending upon the dumpster
Cart my furniture away
Each according to his and her ability.
Mattress, table, mop handle, garbage bag.
What do I want...
To be a family? Their laughter is a place.
I have cleaned out a room—
Pine Sol, Murphy's Oil—
While lilacs pierce May through.
And I don't need to touch the wound.

Aubade

We used up everything in that hotel
where we were first lovers,
then borrowed extra from the afterlife.

Workers will excavate
the ottoman to which we fed
all our pillows. We preferred to

stretch out against the riverbed,
faces to silt. Sleeping like
hoofprints after deer

before the water rushes back. Now
I know what was being built.
What we saw partially and remarked on

that cold morning. The high-rise
scaffold going up. Breezy Tyvek.
Sharp planks symmetrical as

ribs, sun hurtling
through them, only seemed—
by some trick of ice and dawn—to be

making a ramp for us. And just beyond:
the golden ship we would leave on.

The Great Conjunction

I wasn't convinced, when we drove to the lake
one night that last winter and pulled over,
that we'd arrived at what the paper told us
not to miss. Jupiter. Saturn. Two blurry dots
almost touching.

The blinking could have been anything—airplanes,
streetlights—but, too, the marriage
was failing. We tried once more to both believe.
The whole city was searching,
but we were somehow in that field alone
peering up at two points suspended over the water.

Fatigued—that's how I see them now—as if
relying on our looking to stay there.
And the Great Conjunction was us trying.

Apostrophe

So often, I've shouted *hello* from a dock.
Water bouncing like light. Sound coming back
in the shape of a heron rising and leaving.

I've driven around calling a man's name—
closed windows blunting the swell—though
he was states away. Scraping my vocal cords

as if one of us was lost in a forest. I've missed
the turn for my own street. And at the end of it,
I know now, if I drive long enough,

yearning opens onto a smooth lake in the dark
where I can set down my questions like lanterns.
From this distance, they could be anyone's.

Panama

Thanks for carrying the air conditioner, and thanks
for taking off my dress.

Thanks for the afternoon light on your chest
when you said *I don't think what we want is that different.*

The week before you proposed, you said *I'm a man with a plan*
and all I could think of was *Panama.*

Thanks for getting me pregnant so many times
in dreams. Thanks for considering

waiting in line at the Met
for Michelangelo's drawings. It was raining that day.

Somebody said—maybe you, maybe the *New York Times,*
that the crowd was so big and the pictures so small, it was

hard to get a good look. So we left without trying.
We went to the farmer's market, and you bought a blue knit hat.

Do you remember? There was a time when we were certain
of our love. We stood looking over Canadaway Creek,

and it wasn't a shadow—that steelhead twisting in the water,
trying but failing to disguise itself against the shale.

Acknowledgments

Thank you to the editors of the following literary magazines, in which versions of poems from this collection first appeared:

At Length: "The Afterlife"
The Baffler: "The Runaway" (as "Mass. Ave"), "Vines"
Cider Press Review: "Arrhythmias"
Copper Nickel: "The Deletions"
Gettysburg Review: "Lost Button"
LEVELER: "The Auditions"
Mid-American Review: "Kanyakumari" (as "Four Leaves")
New Ohio Review: "The Great Conjunction"
The Paris Review: "Vortex, Amtrak"
Pioneer Works: "Matter," "Aubade," "Apostrophe," "Panama"
Pleiades: "Lorain County, 1999," "Tinder"
Ploughshares: "Boston Harbor"
Sixth Finch: "Ursa Major," "Nike," "Lines on Trees," and "My Liver"
32 Poems: "Stick Figure," "Blueberries for Sal"

Enormous thank you to Mary Biddinger for selecting my manuscript as the Editor's Choice and Akron Poetry Prize Judge Sandra Beasley for her early feedback on the collection. Thanks to the literary journal editors who chose to give homes to this work along the way, including Mark Drew, Wayne Miller, Jenny Molberg, George David Clark, David Wanczyk, Mark Halliday, Michael Shewmaker, John Skoyles, Nicole Terez Dutton, and Rob MacDonald. Thank you to the Vermont Studio Center for the residency. And to VSC comrade Kylie Gellatly for the powerful cover photo.

Additional gratitude to the following humans for their role in the development of the poems and/or significant moral support throughout the project: Kiese Laymon, Katie Ford, Josh Aiken, Chelsea DesAutels, Kathryn Savage, Claire Wahmanholm, Susie Emmert, Kelly Smith, Ross Gay, Natalie Shapero, Jill McDonough, Meg Day, Katie Peterson, Anne Valente, Maggie Smith, Jason Reed, Katie Hays, Jen Moore, Martha Collins, Marianne Boruch, Maggie Messitt, Joshua T. Anderson, Christie Towers, Mike Dando, Nomi Stone, Andrew Collard, Judith Dorn, Josh Raisler Cohn, Nathaniel Raymond, Russell Linville, and Quinn Garner.

Thanks to the Run Minnesota Polar Bears.

A Note on the Cover Art

Before moving away from my hometown in 2008, I photographed some dozen houses to create a ghostly portrait of home and memory. After several years and many more moves, the print was housed in a storage unit in Johnson, Vermont, when the water found it. In 2023, the Lamoille River rose in a historic flood, disrupting many lives and destroying countless homes. The storage unit filled with water and left this, and many other pieces of art, in an altered—collaborated—state. When the waters receded, the erratic behavior of the rising river left the trace of its movement in the inks of this photograph, reading as an homage to the many homes and lives affected by the flood.

Kylie Gellatly
http://www.kyliegellatly.com

Photo: Zoe Prinds-Flash

Sarah Green is the author of a previous collection, *Earth Science* (421 Atlanta), and the editor of *Welcome to the Neighborhood: An Anthology of American Coexistence* (Ohio University Press.) She has received a Pushcart Prize and fellowships from the Sewanee Writers' Conference and the Vermont Studio Center. She is an associate professor of English and Creative Writing at St. Cloud State University.